It's All Love

REFLECTIONS
— FOR YOUR —
HEART & SOUL

JENNA ORTEGA

RANDOM HOUSE 🏠 NEW YORK

Library of Congress Cataloging-in-Publication Data is available upon request.
ISBN 978-0-593-17456-2 (trade) — ISBN 978-0-593-17457-9 (lib. bdg.) —
ISBN 978-0-593-17458-6 (ebook)

The text of this book is set in 10.8-point Sabon MT Pro.
Interior design by Cathy Bobak

Printed in the United States of America
10 9 8 7 6 5 4
First Edition

For my mom, who inspires everything I do

CONTENTS

I interact with the world from a place of love and light. I see my own story in so many of those who reach out to me on social media or stop me on the street to share their struggles. I connect with supporters whose languages, lifestyles, and faiths differ greatly from mine—yet, despite everything we don't have in common, we connect as people who face the same doubts and insecurities, who want to look in the mirror and find love in our reflections. I've led a blessed life in many ways, but I've also faced plenty of hard times. When I see a message from a follower about feeling lonely or not believing in their power, I identify. Because I've felt it, too. I want you, my readers, to know that you are not alone. We're all more alike than most of us realize. We're in this together. It's all love.

It's my greatest hope that the honesty and heart I've poured into these pages will bring some love and some light into your life. There's so much I want to say about the power within us all to be kind to each other, to lift each other up, to be gracious with ourselves as we grow on this journey. I'm sharing intimate, personal stories about embracing confidence and self-worth, taking chances, and working through stress and anxiety. I hope, by sharing my experiences and the advice I have from going through these situations myself, that I can help you face them.

I have been fortunate to be able to follow my passion for acting and do what I love every day. It took a lot of courage and determination to put myself out there in the business, to strive for roles I wasn't sure about, to count myself as a worthy choice for big projects. The idea of failing can be scary, but betting on yourself is beyond worthwhile. We're all on our own journeys. It's easy to compare myself to others, and it can be tough for me to appreciate my success and my hard-earned progress toward my goals when others are on their own (sometimes faster) trajectories. To honor your passions, to be confident in what you have to say and offer the world, to let go of fear, jealousy, and self-doubt—these are the most difficult things we can do. It's a practice, one that we have to live every day. Sometimes we win, and sometimes we don't. But we can always wake up the next morning ready to try again. Never let your fears stop you from working toward your dreams. You are in charge of your story.

All my love,
Jenna

LIVE WITH LOVE

EVERYTHING

I DO

IS DRIVEN

BY LOVE.

The way I interact with the world comes from a place of love and light. I've learned not to criticize, get caught up in negative energy, or speak badly about others. On subjects I'm passionate about and involved in, I speak out in a positive way to bring people together to discuss important issues without hatred. And when I feel less informed about a topic, I make sure to educate myself.

When I'm working, I try to bring love and positivity to the set with me every day. I love my craft, and I'm so grateful that I get to follow my passion. I let that love pour out in small ways and big ways: doing nice, thoughtful things for the people I'm working with goes a long way. Early mornings, late nights, and long days are often challenging, but they never get the best of me. I always remember how grateful I am just to be working. It's all a privilege.

PRIORITIZE
KINDNESS.

A costar once pointed out to me that every time I interact with someone new on set, I pay them a compliment. At first, I worried it meant I was being a suck-up. But I realized that when I was in a very dark place in my life and someone would compliment me, even if it was about something small like my shoes, it would lift me up. I internalized that lesson, and I look for something to appreciate in another person when we first connect. You never know if someone is having a bad day, and maybe a small compliment will help bring them a smile. It can feel good just to be noticed.

I only want to do kind things because anything else is a waste of time and a waste of energy. Being mean doesn't improve your state of mind. Why not look for something positive?

SET THE SAME STANDARDS
FOR YOURSELF
THAT YOU WOULD SET
FOR YOUR BEST FRIEND
OR YOUR SISTER.
NEVER SETTLE.

I encourage my friends to focus on the personality traits of their crushes, not just looks. Someone who can challenge you intellectually and teach you something new about yourself is someone you can build a friendship with. The best relationships are always built on friendship first. Rather than get carried away by the attention or an initial attraction, I remind myself to really get to know someone. Trustworthiness, optimism, and a good sense of humor are very attractive to me. Life is stressful, so I need someone to help me feel good and see the positive. I also find kindness the most attractive quality in a guy. When I like someone, I want to see how he treats others who have nothing to give him in return, whether he's kind for the sake of being kind.

I BELIEVE THAT SOME
PEOPLE ARE MEANT
TO BE IN YOUR LIFE
FOR A REASON. YOU CAN
HAVE MORE THAN
ONE SOUL MATE.

I am lucky to have a group of best friends who have grown up with me. One of my closest girlfriends and I recently connected on a deeper level, with long conversations about the universe, politics and social justice, our futures, and how quickly adulthood is coming upon us. We share opinions about the things that matter, and we have the same dry and sarcastic sense of humor. I feel like I can talk about things with her that I can't talk about with many other people. She offers me a nonjudgmental place to talk during tough or stressful times. I'm blessed to have a friend who understands and connects with me so deeply. I truly can't imagine my life without her. She knows me, sees me, supports and appreciates me, and loves me unconditionally. How else would you describe a soul mate?

BE PATIENT
WITH A
BROKEN HEART.

When you lose someone you love, it's hard to separate yourself from the emotions and the memories. Healing is a process, and it doesn't happen overnight. A relationship is only between you and that other person: nobody else will truly understand what it meant to you, and nobody else can know for sure when it's time for you to move on.

Just as it's important to cherish and respect your memories, it's even more important to remember that you need to go out and make new ones. Continue to live life! When you are too focused on the past, you can get stuck there. Sometimes I'll see a friend get so wrapped up in grieving the end of a relationship, they forget to go out with friends and make new memories. Try not to hold on to things that keep you stuck in the past. I'm not saying that you have to spend hours scrubbing your Instagram! But don't clutter your space with mementos or photos, either. Those ties to the past will just hold you back.

YOU LEARN AS MUCH
FROM THE BAD
RELATIONSHIPS AS FROM
THE GOOD ONES.

I'm grateful for every relationship in my life, good and bad, because they've all contributed to my growth. Sometimes the tough relationships end up teaching you more than the beautiful ones, as difficult as those lessons can be.

There was a girl I became friends with in middle school. She was new in town, so I took her under my wing and introduced her to my friends. She was so sweet at first, but it wasn't long before she showed her true colors. I was devastated! She caused problems among my closest friendships for no clear reason. Ever since, I've been cautious about who I let into my inner social circle, and I'm open and direct if any issues come up with a friend. It's made me appreciate my true friendships even more.

NEVER DOUBT
YOUR ABILITY TO LOVE
OTHERS AND YOUR ABILITY
TO BE LOVED.

Everyone has insecurities, and many people have moments when they feel they're not worthy of love. Believe me, I've been there. When I feel really insecure and low, I tend to isolate myself from the people I love most so that I won't drag them down. My insecurities act as a wall. But then I think about my family and my close friends, about how amazing they are, and wonder what I did to deserve them. And you know what I've learned? Those insecure, low moments happen exactly when I need them most.

TRUST YOUR FRIENDS
WHEN THEY TELL YOU
WHAT THEY SEE IN YOU,
AND REFLECT THEIR OWN
GOODNESS BACK
TO THEM.

When I'm feeling overly critical of myself, I trust my friends and family and their love for me. If they care enough to support me and love me, I have to trust there's something they see in me, even if I can't see it in myself. You don't need a ton of people in your world just a few important ones to reflect your value and give you peace when you can't find it for yourself.

I DON'T BELIEVE IN
LOVE AT FIRST SIGHT.
I BELIEVE IN LOVE
AFTER BUILDING
TRUST AND FRIENDSHIP.

Love at first sight sounds so exciting: sweet and innocent and pure. But love, for me, is something you build through trust and connection. It's a journey you go on with somebody. You don't start at the finish line. For me, love is knowing someone's going to be by your side through the ups and downs. It's built over time, maybe starting with that early infatuation, and then growing a friendship as you get to know each other. That's what leads to love.

DON'T MISTAKE

INFATUATION

FOR LOVE.

I *do* believe in infatuation at first sight—infatuation is so powerful! It can cloud your judgment and lead you to trust someone more than you should. I'm a sucker for a good sense of humor and guys who are passionate about their talents. I respect someone who works on their craft, whatever it is. While those qualities are really attractive to me and get my attention right away, I've had to learn the difference between love and infatuation.

I've taught myself how to slow down that initial attraction and really get to know someone before jumping in. It's easy to meet someone and dive into the fantasy of being with them. I try to limit how much I think about someone new, to stay firmly rooted in reality. I don't check out his social media to learn more about him. I have the discipline to back off and let whatever is going to happen happen. It might take a few tries, but you can do the same thing. I also focus on the love I have for my family and my friends, and I compare that to my feelings for a guy to remind myself that dating is not as intense as it may seem.

IF YOU LOOK FOR THE
NEGATIVE, THAT'S WHAT
YOU'RE GOING TO FIND.
SEEK OUT THE POSITIVE
AND LET YOURSELF
BE AMAZED.

As somebody who's dealt with a lot of disappointing people and situations, I am working on this every day. I got to a point where I built a wall to protect myself. But when you build walls, you block out the good along with the bad. I think it's important to give people the benefit of the doubt, to give them the chance to show you who they are and what they're about. That doesn't mean opening up to a new person right away and divulging your deepest, darkest secrets—it means being receptive to the idea that somebody else could understand you. I'll always be a little cautious and protective, but I want to be open to new people and new friendships. I want to let myself be pleasantly surprised by new friendships and interesting perspectives.

I TRY TO KEEP
THE WORD *HATE* OUT
OF MY VOCABULARY.

I can't tell you how much I dislike the word *hate*. When I was in a dark place and feeling really down on myself, it was a word I used often. I didn't like the way I felt, and I would act downright mean toward other people.

Thankfully I've realized that wallowing in self-doubt wasn't good for me. I actually started to change for the better when I told myself never to use the word *hate* again. What we say to others, and especially what we say to ourselves, affects our emotional state and our energy. Now I try to stick to lighter words and lighter ways of being because I want to surround myself with light and positivity and love. I believe that you manifest what you put into the world.

In the last few years, I've learned to reframe my negative thoughts into positive ones, or at least less negative ones. If I am looking in the mirror and feel myself about to pick out a flaw, I replace that thought with one rooted in appreciation or neutrality. Or if I'm going to an audition or an event, or even a workout class, that I'm dreading, I remind myself why I signed up—I trust that my past self knew what she was doing and jump into whatever I'm doing with confidence.

EVEN YOUR STRONGEST
OPINIONS AND VIEWS MAY
CHANGE OVER TIME.

Life is constantly evolving, and your view of the world will change as you get older. You should embrace this process rather than fight it. People change, and it's only natural that your take on certain things will change with you. We should all continue to educate ourselves, talk to new people, and seek out new information. Let's embrace the idea that the day we stop learning, we stop growing. And I want to be continually learning, growing, and improving. Each of our perspectives is based on our memories and ideas and conversations. It's important that you have an open mind and know there's so much more to experience and learn.

KEEP THE FAITH

WHATEVER YOU CALL
YOUR HIGHER POWER,
WHATEVER TYPE OF PRAYER
OR PRACTICE INSPIRES
YOU, WE ARE CONNECTED
IN OUR FAITH.

Faith is unique to each person, but it provides a great connection to the world and the universe around us. Faith is not necessarily the same as religion, although they're often used interchangeably. If you don't have a strong religious practice or an affiliation with a certain religious sect, you can still be faithful. Faith is also belief, and that belief can be in God, or in the goodness of the universe around you, or maybe even in yourself. It's a foundation to stand on when things get hard.

MY FAITH GAVE ME
SOMETHING TO BELIEVE IN
WHEN I DIDN'T BELIEVE
IN MYSELF.

What I've learned on Sunday mornings inspires me in everything I do. My faith inspires me to believe in myself when I feel doubts and insecurities creeping in. When I pray, I'm reminded of the strength of my family and our shared convictions, and how much they love and support me. I've grown so much within the context of my faith, and it's been a source of encouragement and inspiration that I've relied on all my life. When I'm feeling down or frustrated about not getting a role, messing up my lines while filming, or a misunderstanding with my friends, I remember to pray to reconnect to God and remind myself there's a greater plan at work. Prayer has been a part of my life for as long as I can remember, and it helps me feel secure when I'm uneasy. I'm the most inspired when I'm connected with my faith. My faith is the root of my love for, and belief in, myself.

PRAYER IS A MANTRA AND
A WAY OF CENTERING
YOURSELF, REGARDLESS OF
WHAT YOU BELIEVE IN.

I stay connected to my faith by praying. I love that prayer can happen wherever you are, whenever you have a spare moment. The more I pray, the less I feel that the universe is against me. You don't have to be religious or believe in one spiritual practice over another. Prayer is a way to slow down and sit quietly with your thoughts. It allows you to connect to yourself and what you're feeling, and to consider what's troubling you, stressing you, or, yes, exciting you. You can offer up your gratitude for your family and friends, or anything you're appreciative of in your life.

OPEN YOUR ARMS IN
ACCEPTANCE OF OTHERS.

The principles of my faith inform who I am every day, especially the way I treat others. The idea of "love thy neighbor as thyself" is important to me and something I try to live by. Right now, everything is so divided in our country. Prejudices against different groups of people for their gender, race, religion, or sexual orientation are tearing us apart. My faith and my religion have given me the mindset of acceptance, and I'm not going to look at anybody else differently because of their belief, their background, or the way they live their life. My faith has helped me stay open-minded, accepting others and treating them with respect even if they've made different choices.

When I say "love thy neighbor as thyself," I'm really saying "come from a place of love." It's about not treating anyone with disrespect for the way they live. I try to value every connection that I make and appreciate the individual and the opportunity to learn from new perspectives. My faith encourages me to educate myself, to hear from people with different religious backgrounds or views.

HOLD YOUR FAITH CLOSE,
ESPECIALLY IN LIFE'S MOST
OVERWHELMING MOMENTS.

The tricky part about faith is that you have to make it a priority. I definitely go through periods where I stray from God's light, forgetting to turn to God. It always happens during times of distraction and work stress, when self-doubt pushes me to my limits. I've realized that letting go of my faith makes me feel worse about myself—more unsure and isolated. But when I prioritize it, everything else falls into place.

While filming season three of *Stuck in the Middle,* my schedule got much busier than usual. I wasn't praying, and I felt disconnected from the world around me. My anxiety was getting worse. Finally, I sat down with my mom and broke down crying. I told her I didn't feel like myself. She made me sit there for ten minutes doing nothing, just breathing. Then she asked what I'd done during those few minutes of silence, and I told her I was thinking about all the things I had to do. She asked, *Why aren't you praying?* That shook me and made me realize that I was allowing myself to lose the solid ground beneath my feet.

I made it a priority to pray every night after that, to hold on to my faith during times of stress. Hard times are inevitable, but I will never again forget to reconnect with my faith.

FAITH CAN BE A LIGHT
THROUGH THE DARKEST
OF TIMES.

I know what it's like to feel the pressure of needing to be perfect. I know what it's like to feel insecure and cautious about everything you say and do.

There was a time when I isolated myself, never taking action. I didn't want to pray because I felt my problems were too small to pray about compared to everything else going on in the world. I was living in Los Angeles, away from my family, and didn't have time to go to church. I didn't know who I could trust. I had so much doubt that I started to question my faith.

On a much-needed break, I went to visit my family, and we all went to church together. The pastor was telling Bible stories I'd heard my whole life, but they took on new meaning in the context of what I was struggling with. I felt like I was at home for the first time in a long time. I was able to take those feelings of comfort and confidence, of identity and belonging, and bring them into my hectic life in LA.

EMBRACE YOUR FAITH
OUT LOUD AND RISK
INSPIRING OTHERS.

When I was in middle school, I became close with a girl who was having a hard time with her parents. They kept fighting and splitting up, then getting back together. It was such a difficult and emotional time for her, and she badly needed comfort. In addition to lending a sympathetic ear, I shared the power and comfort of my faith.

It's a very vulnerable thing to share the depth of your faith and what it means to you, but I'm glad to have shared in that way. My friend was open, and the way I talked about my faith seemed to give her hope. She wanted to know more about God and what I got out of my faith practices. I brought her to church with my family a few times, and she really connected with it. In those moments when she needed support and needed to feel connected, she found it in faith.

IT'S ALL IN
GOD'S TIMING.

As an actor, I put myself in competitive situations all the time, and it can be devastating to lose out on a role. I remember one big opportunity when I was up for a role in a more mature comedy/action family movie starring two young actors who are huge stars. The project was with a director I wanted to work with, and when I did a chemistry read with the lead actor, it felt like everything clicked.

But it wasn't meant to be.

Oh, how I cried when I got the news! And my mom cried with me. I took a minute to sit with it, but if it wasn't meant to be, it wasn't meant to be. I knew I would get the chance to do more adult, serious roles when I was ready, and before too long, I did. Things may happen more quickly for others, but it's all in God's timing. Now I don't cry over roles. If something doesn't go my way, I reassure myself that it's all God's plan, and I'll get the right role when it's the right time.

I BELIEVE
IN THE DEPTH
OF MY FAITH.

It's nice to believe in something even when you don't believe in yourself. When you're in a dark place, I suggest trying to hold on to the things that give you hope, whether that's supportive people in your life, your religion, or your ability to do good work. It's so important to gravitate toward the things that keep you grounded, connected, and inspired. Those will definitely pull you out of your slump. My faith reminds me who I am and gives me a connection to members of my church community and believers at large. I lean on my faith to reassure me and give me hope.

LIFE WON'T ALWAYS GO
THE WAY YOU WANT.
EMBRACE IT ANYWAY.

I've learned that life is unpredictable and it's so much healthier to let go and have faith that it will work out the way it's meant to. Anytime I'm scared and start to let myself get wrapped up in worst-case-scenario thinking, my faith keeps me anchored. Faith helps me let go of what I can't control. As long as I know that I did everything I could, my faith reassures me when doubt creeps in. This is a particularly comforting thought for me, because I often feel the need to control everything, from social situations to the trajectory of my career, and if something doesn't go the way I want it to, it can ignite my anxiety.

WE WERE ALL PUT ON THE
PLANET WITH A PURPOSE.

There were so many paths I could have gone down, so many things I was interested in. But I was drawn to acting from a young age: sharing stories and creating characters that connect and maybe even inspire audiences. Through stories, through laughter, through entertainment, I have had the chance to spread the love and light that is so important to me. Acting has given me the platform and opportunity to use my voice for good—to increase awareness of worthy causes and share empowering advice with my fans. If something doesn't work out like you want it to, it's because that's not your purpose yet and you'll find it eventually. Just have faith.

PRAY WITH AN OPEN HEART
AND TRUE INTENTIONS.

Whenever people tell me to pray for something that will benefit me, I always get honest with myself and identify my true intentions first. I've witnessed so many people go through the motions of being religious and praying but not be truly invested. Prayer is a way to broaden your faith through deep conversation and understanding. I try to pray from a place of authenticity and gratitude, to adopt an open mind in my search for guidance.

When I was younger, my mom encouraged me and my siblings to pray every night. It became something I took for granted. I began praying for things that didn't really matter, like a new pair of shoes or a good grade on a test. It became a wish list. My mom reminded me one day that I didn't have to ask for anything when I prayed. I could simply have a conversation with God. For the next month, I set a goal to pray every morning and every evening. I told God about my day, shared my highs and lows, and considered what I needed guidance on. By the end of that month, I felt closer to God than ever.

APPRECIATE
YOUR FAMILY

MY FAMILY

IS THE FOUNDATION

OF MY STORY.

So often we're focused on material things and superficial problems, but at the end of the day, life is all about your family—by blood or by choice. My family is everything to me, and my parents and siblings are there for me like no one else, listening and supporting me and reminding me who I am and where I came from. I have two older sisters, one older brother, one younger brother, and one younger sister—between the six of us, I've heard it *all*. We talk about everything, from knowing when to take a chance in your career to knowing if a guy is playing games. I don't spend as much time with my family as I'd like because I'm often working and I can only make the trip back home every few months. Even though we're apart, I'm constantly texting and calling, and I use FaceTime to check in. It's so important to me to stay connected. But nothing beats coming home for a few days, resting, hanging out with everyone, playing soccer, and going to church.

FAMILY CAN BE
ANYTHING
YOU WANT IT
TO BE.

You have your blood relatives, but it's also important to build a family of friends who can be there for you when your other family is far away or inaccessible. Just because your friends aren't related to you by blood doesn't make them any less meaningful. Since I'm away from my family so much, I built a family in LA that I truly love and know will be in my life forever. My core group of friends, whom I met during my first few years working in television, are the people I turn to when I need tough-love advice on subjects like heartbreak and career stress, and even the bigger existential crises on occasion. My stylist, Enrique Melendez, is like a protective big brother, always looking out for me. My *Stuck in the Middle* castmate Isaak Presley and his dad, Lou, are also like family to me. And, of course, Kayla Maisonet is like a sister, there to vent and commiserate. We've spent so much time together talking about the pressures of our careers. They're there to cry, laugh, run wild, and hold me when my family feels too far away.

LEARN TO ACCEPT HELP
AND SACRIFICE FROM
YOUR FAMILY, AND TRUST
THAT THEY'RE ACTING
OUT OF LOVE.

Whenever I start to question my career, I think about what my family is giving up so that I can pursue my dream. My mom balances a lot between my career, her own job, and our family's demands. She has done so much and has been such a source of strength for me—and all of my siblings—that I feel like I'll never be able to express my gratitude properly. If my family is okay with the way things are, then all I can do is be grateful for their selfless support and do my best with what I can control. It can be tough to learn to accept help and sacrifice from your family, and trust that they're acting out of love. I know I would do absolutely anything for my family, and it's beautiful to know they would do the same.

THERE'S NOTHING LIKE

THE BOND

BETWEEN SISTERS.

No matter where I am in life, I know my sisters are always there for me. They're like built-in best friends. We will be together forever and have each other's backs, even when we don't see eye to eye. I can tell my sisters anything. I know I can call, text, or FaceTime any of them to share what's going on with me, vent about frustrations, or dish about gossip and crushes. Do you know how many conversations I've had with my sisters about whether a guy is worth my time? *A lot.* We're different in many ways, and yet we support each other, no matter what. I'm so grateful that my sisters will come to me with their problems, and I try to be there as a sounding board with lots of empathy and advice.

TRADITIONS BUILD
MEMORIES, LOVE, AND
CONSISTENCY.

In Latinx culture, there's an emphasis on staying connected to family traditions. In part, it's a way to honor relatives who have passed. I realize that's not everyone's thing, but we hold on to traditions for the history, and also because they're fun. I love that I can count on our traditions throughout the year, and I find comfort in celebrating holidays and cooking meals together, whether it's tamales every Christmas, a huge extended family reunion every Easter, or birthdays celebrated as a family. Our traditions keep us grounded—no matter how much we change or what difficulties we face, we can always come back to those familiar touchstones and feel the love.

FAMILY MEANS
PRIORITIZING
SOMEONE ELSE'S
HAPPINESS AND
WELL-BEING.

Sometimes, when I consider the depth of the love and appreciation I have for my family, I'm overwhelmed by it. In those moments when my love for them just amazes me, I know I would do anything for them. Their happiness is so important to me. I'm sure that's how my parents feel about all of us, and I'm so blessed to be a part of my family.

Prioritizing the happiness of family, and even close friends, over your own is a noble, selfless quality . . . to a point. It can also be taxing. I'm so happy that my friends or siblings can come to me and feel comfortable enough to ask for help with their problems. But I also put so much energy into being there for other people that I sometimes don't take good care of myself. I'm working on learning how to be selective with where I put my energy. As much as I want to be there for everyone, it's not possible or healthy to be that emotionally available all the time.

FAMILIES AREN'T PERFECT,
BUT THEY'RE OFTEN
ACCIDENTALLY BEAUTIFUL.

With family, you may not always get along, and certainly we're all flawed in our own way. Everybody is dealing with their own stress and insecurities, trying to get to the end of the day or the week as gracefully as possible. But no matter what's going on, my family will always be there. The way we love and support each other unconditionally is so affirming. It doesn't matter what type of family you have, and it certainly doesn't have to be traditional or biological to be valuable.

ALL RELATIONSHIPS HAVE
THEIR UPS AND DOWNS—
INCLUDING RELATIONSHIPS
WITH FAMILY.

No one is perfect, and sometimes even siblings can disagree, drift apart, and find themselves on different paths. It can be heartbreaking and frustrating, but we have to remember that families love each other and are connected in a way that cannot be broken. Right now, my older brother and I aren't on the best terms. I haven't seen him in almost a year, which is the longest we've ever gone. We got into an argument last year about prioritizing family, actually. When he does reach out, it doesn't seem like he's really interested in talking to me; rather, he has his own agenda. As time goes on, more milestones and events pass us by. But even so, I know without a doubt that we still love each other and would do anything for each other. Sometimes the best thing for us is to love our family members from a distance, as painful as it is.

WHERE YOU'RE FROM
IS JUST A PLACE.
HOME IS WHERE
YOUR FAMILY IS.

As much as I love the desert where I'm from, and as much as my family home holds sentimental value, it's just a place. Home is where my family is, where I feel unconditionally accepted and loved and challenged to be my best, true self. If I'm on set or working on location anywhere from California to Spain to Asia, and my family comes to visit, I'm home. My parents and siblings and chosen family, people who understand me better than I understand myself, are all I need to be at ease in any space. Home is where your people are, where you're comfortable and feel safe and loved because you're with them.

FAMILY IS ONE OF THE
BIGGEST INFLUENCES ON
WHO WE BECOME.

Family is the foundation of who you are, and it influences how you see the world in so many ways. My family absolutely shaped my values and beliefs. I want to make them proud, and that informs how I treat people and carry myself. On the flip side, I've seen friends who have tough relationships with their families or had challenging childhoods take those experiences and use them to become even stronger and more resilient and compassionate. As I get older and meet more people, my world becomes bigger. I feel like everybody I interact with influences my life and my character in some way. These experiences strengthen the already-strong foundation my family has instilled in me.

CERTAIN FRIENDS

WILL COME AND GO.

FAMILY IS FOREVER.

However you define your "family"—whether it's immediate or extended family, or friends who have become family—they will always be there for you. I could screw up big-time, but family will stay beside me, whereas friends may walk away. When you go through storms in life, you really understand how much family matters. They're the people who drop everything and rush to help you pick up the pieces when you need them most. I'm luckier than many people when it comes to my family, and I thank God every day for them.

TAKE CHANCES

TAKING CHANCES
IS THE ONLY WAY
TO BE GREAT.

The beauty of life is in the unknown, and you never know what you can accomplish until you try. It can be scary and uncomfortable to put yourself out there, but taking risks is how you push yourself to new heights.

Actors have to cry on demand, but after working on a Disney show for so many years, I was out of practice. When I started filming season two of *You*, I knew I would have to cry. And it wasn't just a simple tear. It was a physical scene, very intense. I stressed about it so much that I had trouble getting into the scene and connecting with the emotions. I was afraid to go all in, embarrassed that my new colleagues would think I was overacting or trying too hard. I respected the actors around me so much that I was worried what they would think of my performance. But when I finally allowed myself to let go and just live in the moment, it went so well. It's the scene I'm proudest of in the entire project.

YOU'RE MOST SUCCESSFUL
WHEN YOU'RE
UNCOMFORTABLE.

With the exception of a small part in a school production of *Peter Pan*, I had no theater experience when I auditioned at Radio City Music Hall. The opportunity for the lead role in *New York Spectacular Starring the Radio City Rockettes* came up, and soon I was on a plane to New York. I love to dance, but I'm not a trained dancer. The other people auditioning had experience on Broadway and seemed much more comfortable learning choreography on the spot. I was like, "Hey, shouldn't we put up a camera and do everything twenty times?" I was so out of my comfort zone, I just had to throw up my hands and give it my all without overthinking it. As if that wasn't stressful enough, the producers had trouble hearing me. I'm pretty quiet, and when you're doing theater, you have to project your voice to the very last row of seats. They asked me to stand in the back of the enormous rehearsal room and get my voice to the other side of the room. I could either overthink everything or let go and go for it. I sang my heart out; I danced with abandon; I projected my voice all the way to the West Coast because that's what they told me to do.

I ended up getting up the part and moving to New York City for three months. The experience was something I wouldn't trade for the world, and it's also the most uncomfortable I have ever been.

I'D RATHER
TRY AND FAIL
THAN NEVER PUT MYSELF
OUT THERE.

Failure, as much as it can suck, is such a crucial part of learning and improving. My mom often reminds me that this is the moment to be making mistakes. I'm young, I'm still learning, and no one is holding me to a perfect standard (except maybe myself). This is the time in our lives to embrace mistakes and use them as tools to get better. There is so much potential in humility and openness. I want to work to be the best person I can be and the best at my craft.

I learned the importance of trying and failing recently when I was up for a huge movie role. I was called back for the second round, and I got too in my head about how big the project was, how visible the role would be, how demanding it would be on my and my family's schedule. I overthought *everything*. I just couldn't stomach the stress, so I thanked everyone and bowed out. Another actress got the role, and it was a huge move for her career. When I saw the finished project, I was impressed with her performance, but I couldn't help wondering what I could have done in the role, how it might have changed my life, what that alternate universe version of the movie would have looked like. Now I know to just take risks and see what happens.

YOU HAVE TO TRY
DIFFERENT THINGS TO
FIGURE OUT WHAT WORKS
BEST FOR YOU.

Actors utilize various backgrounds or techniques to strengthen their performances. These modes of working, of acting, encompass a huge range of skills. There's the Meisner technique, which requires being completely out of your head so that you can react solely on instinct. There's also method acting, which is when you're so in the character's head that you act like the character even when the cameras aren't rolling, and you try to inhabit their life completely. I've learned so much from observing the talented people I work with. Penn Badgley is an incredible actor who I loved working with on *You*. He's so relaxed and easygoing when the cameras are off, and his mannerisms on camera are flawless and natural. I appreciate watching and learning from other people, because you never know what will click for your own craft.

Trial and error is one of the best ways to learn. It does require time and patience, though. I've seen actors use techniques I'm not used to seeing, and I've tried them myself. It's a good way to diversify my acting skills and find out how many different ways I can get a performance I'm happy with. Once, I tried a new method in a scene, and the director came over to me and said, "Jenna, I don't know what you're doing, but that's not it!" *Okay, then!* I quickly regrouped and ditched that particular technique in favor of my more familiar method.

NEVER BE AFRAID
TO MAKE MISTAKES.
IT'S ALL PART OF
THE CREATIVE PROCESS.

One of the best ways to get to know yourself is to try new things. When you put yourself out there and do different activities, you learn more about what you like and dislike and might even find something you're passionate about.

It's good to be able to sing as an actress, and when I was younger, I loved to sing. (I even entered my school's talent show in the fourth grade.) When I used to take singing lessons, I trained with a lot of musical theater songs because they strengthen your vocal cords—which gave me an appreciation for musical theater. Taking those classes led me to value music on a broader scale and educated me about a whole new world in my profession.

The older I get, the more I realize that singing is ultimately not something I enjoy doing anymore, but I firmly believe that you should try as many new things as possible and practice allowing yourself to be creative and free.

SOMETIMES
LESS IS MORE.

Producers give feedback in the audition room, so you have to give yourself space to adapt your performance and work on their notes. If I'm too in my head, if I'm too locked into how I've rehearsed, I can't adapt to the feedback in the room. This practice has translated well into other areas of my life where I'm prone to overthinking and trying to control everything. When it comes to meeting new people, taking chances on a new project or business relationship, or preparing for a role, I try to listen to my instincts, too. Be prepared, yes, but also let yourself be you.

IT'S IMPORTANT TO
FORGIVE, BUT THAT
DOESN'T MEAN
YOU HAVE TO FORGET.

It's not good to hold on to anger and negative energy after a fight with a friend or a love. It's better to let it go and repair the relationship, or move on from it. But never forget the lessons you learn in the process.

When a boy I was talking to started coming on too strong, I told him that I felt uncomfortable. I'd made it clear we were just friends, but *he* kept making it clear he wanted more. I tried to make it as. clear. as. possible. that I wasn't interested in being romantic with him, but he kept on with the advances. That's when I decided that I needed to end the friendship. I knew my judgment of him was accurate, and I needed to follow my intuition.

THERE ARE ALWAYS

GOING TO BE HATERS.

A couple of years ago I was at this Disney party in LA, and I ran into another actress I knew. I don't know what she had against me, but she was so confrontational, looking to instigate an argument over anything. I would say something, and she would say the opposite. Later on, when Skai Jackson walked in, we chatted before she went to say hi to the other girl. I looked over and this girl was whispering in Skai's ear while looking directly at me. Skai wouldn't talk to me for the rest of the night. Months later, Skai and I finally sat down and hashed it out. We realized that this girl, who neither of us knew that well, was trying to sabotage our friendship. We've been good friends ever since. Isn't it funny that the same juvenile, petty stuff can happen in middle school *and* in Hollywood?

You don't even have to do anything to a person for them not to like you. Whatever they have against you is about them, not you. Other people have insecurities, and they might not be totally happy. I suggest including them in your prayers, sending them love, and trying to feel empathy for whatever they're going through.

THERE'S NO GROWTH
WITHOUT PAIN.

I've always been afraid of taking risks. And yet the career I've chosen involves a lot of risk taking! If you don't get out there and have new experiences, you're never going to learn anything and you're never going to grow. Whether it's a tough relationship or a professional setback, I've learned from every experience I've had, good and bad.

A few years back, a guy I was dating did something that betrayed my trust, and it caught me by surprise. As tough as that experience was at the time—and believe me when I say I was very upset and hurt—I'm so grateful for it now. I learned the value of trusting my instincts. I had been getting a weird vibe from him and he'd said some shady things, like how he liked "keeping options open" when it comes to relationships. Despite my reservations, I'd let my guard down. I'd pushed away that inner voice warning me that something wasn't right. I've held on to that lesson ever since.

EMBRACE
YOUR MISTAKES.

I've been a perfectionist for as long as I can remember. I can still recall a math test I took in second grade, where I got one question wrong. It was the first time in my life that I didn't get a perfect score, and I spent much of the day crying. My mom had to give me a talking-to, reminding me that not everything's going to be perfect all the time. That lesson was essential for me to learn, and it's one I still hold close.

I make mistakes all the time, and I've learned to handle them with grace. More than that, though, I do my best to learn from them. When I started out as an actress and messed up a line while filming a scene, I used to panic and freak out. Since then, I've worked on handling my mistakes more calmly. I ask myself, *What lesson can I take away from that?* In some cases, I change how I perform the scene, or I deliver the line in a different way. Sometimes it's even better than the first time.

MAKE SURE THAT YOU'RE
AS READY AS POSSIBLE
FOR ANYTHING THAT
COULD HAPPEN.

I've learned a lot about preparation, and I put in the hard work to show up each day ready to do my best. As I'm rehearsing, I come up with fifty different ways to say my lines so that I have options to call on in the moment. I also started doing vocal exercises and warm-ups so that my mouth is more ready. (It sounds silly, but talking all day really does a number on you!) The little mistakes I've made along the way have taught me how to prepare better and have helped me take more risks with my performances. I use them to my advantage, so that the next time, I'm well prepared and confident even if I make a mistake.

I BELIEVE
IN SECOND CHANCES.
WE ALL DESERVE
THE OPPORTUNITY
TO LEARN FROM
OUR MISTAKES.

We're constantly changing and evolving, and we all deserve the chance to improve. The person I was three years ago is very different from the person I am now because I learn more about myself and the world around me every day. That's true of everyone, no matter how old they are. We're all learning and exploring, and figuring out who we are and what works. No one's perfect, and we're all just doing our best. When you don't give someone a second chance and you hold on to a grudge, you clutch that negative energy closer to your body. I don't like to waste time or energy on negativity like that. If a friend makes a mistake and learns from it, if she's able to reevaluate and improve, I give her a lot of respect and move forward with our friendship. Isn't that the least we can ask of anyone? Whenever I make a mistake and learn from it, I hope the other person will give me that same chance.

CHALLENGE
THE STATUS QUO.
YOU ARE IN CONTROL
OF YOUR STORY.
WITH HARD WORK
AND DETERMINATION,
YOUR VISION
FOR YOURSELF
CAN BECOME REALITY.

It's against all odds that I won the role of Harley: I was auditioning for a character described as having blond hair and blue eyes, and at the first audition, I was the only brown person in the room. But before anyone was cast, Disney Channel decided they needed to work on the script and put the auditions on hold.

Soon after, Disney invited me to a workshop for up-and-coming actors to work on developing scripts and perform in front of Disney executives. When they gave us the *Stuck in the Middle* script, I knew it could be my chance to land the role! They had even changed the character's ethnicity. However, I was paired with a girl who was asked to read the role of Harley, while I was asked to play her brother. But I figured if I did a good job reading as the brother, maybe they'd cast me in the next show. Imagine my surprise when casting began again and they asked me to audition for Harley. My hard work and willingness to throw myself into another role got me invited back.

Even though there was a racial barrier at first, I persisted and proved myself. I earned that spot. With dedication and determination, your vision for yourself can become reality. Take the criticism, the slammed doors, and the lack of encouragement and use them as fuel.

PRIORITIZE
YOURSELF

TAKING A MOMENT TO
APPRECIATE
YOUR BLESSINGS
CHANGES EVERYTHING.

My mother raised us not to complain. A cousin of mine who I'm really close with became sick very suddenly when we were younger. She had to spend a lot of time in the hospital, and it was touch and go for a while. Fortunately, she survived, for which we were all so grateful. One night, after I'd spent the day visiting her in the hospital, I looked around the table. Every member of my immediate family was sitting there, healthy and happy. And I was going to school and seeing my friends, and getting to pursue my dream of acting. I needed to take more moments like that, to appreciate my blessings and everything I had. Once I did, I became a happier and more grounded person.

NEVER LET GO OF WHAT
INSPIRES YOU.

When I'm feeling down or lost, I like to journal. Writing has long been both a comfort and a creative outlet for me. I recently found a book of my old essays from school, and it made me proud to remember how much I'd loved writing it and putting it together. When you're down, revisit what connects you to your childhood or your family. It's like going to a favorite childhood spot or seeing an old friend. It opens up great memories and inspires you to create new ones.

Now, whenever I'm sad, I'll get out a notebook and start writing whatever comes to mind, from inspirational thoughts, to journal entries, to short stories. It always makes me feel creative and reminds me who I am at my core.

WHEN YOU'RE TOO BUSY

PLEASING OTHERS,

YOU FORGET TO

PLEASE YOURSELF.

I'm very much a people pleaser, and when I was younger, I often put others' happiness before my own. When I was twelve, I was booked for a magazine photo shoot, one of my first ever. I was super excited. But when I arrived and the stylists pulled out the mood board and showed me outfits, I knew it wouldn't be the experience I'd imagined. The outfits were not my style at all, and I didn't feel comfortable wearing them. The clothes were very girlie—lots of pink, florals, ruffles, and fur, with very high heels. It didn't represent me.

When the photos came out in the magazine weeks later, I saw them and cried. My family was frustrated with me. My siblings said, *Why did you let them tell you to wear those outfits?* I clearly should have said something in the moment. I'd been afraid that they'd be mad at me, but for all I know they would have worked with me to create something I would have been proud of. At every opportunity, represent yourself well and know what you're comfortable doing.

WORK HARD, AND
REST HARD.

I'm seventeen, and I think I can handle everything on my own. But prioritizing rest is a challenge for me, and I have to listen to my mom when she reminds me to take some time for myself. In the last few months, I have been working with a busy, hectic schedule, and my mom saw that it was taking a toll on me. She called my best friend, Kayla, and made plans for us to hang out—to go to the gym and then out to dinner—on one of my days off. After spending time with Kayla and getting those endorphins from our workout, the stress I'd been carrying for months disappeared. I hadn't even known I was *that* stressed out, but my mom knew.

Give yourself time to rest. It's as important as your to-do list. Often when I'm doing so much, I felt guilty resting. But I've finally learned that balance is key.

ASKING FOR HELP

IS A SIGN OF

TRUE STRENGTH.

Many of us try to be strong and stoic, unwilling to admit something's wrong. While going through a really difficult time in my life, it took me a full year to say I needed help to get through it.

For months I had been feeling sad, critical of myself, and apathetic about things that usually got me excited. Then I started having trouble getting out of bed, brushing my hair, getting dressed—I felt there was no point. It's discouraging to feel you're just going through the motions of life. My parents encouraged me to see a therapist, but I refused, thinking I was being a drama queen. I blamed myself for not being stronger or more resilient.

Then came the night I was lying in bed alone, crying for what felt like no reason. I grabbed my journal to see what I'd written over the last year. Rereading my entries, I saw how heartbreakingly sad they were. It was a wake-up call.

When I finally went to a therapist and she used the term *depression*, it felt like a gut punch. It became real in that moment. I also felt great relief that I didn't have to worry I was being dramatic—I was dealing with a mental illness. It was scary to think about, but empowering to give it a name. Even after the first therapy session, and in spite of how uncomfortable I was opening up, I was glad I was doing something.

CHASE THE SMALL
MOMENTS IN LIFE.
MAKE TIME TO FIND
THE BEAUTY AND
PEACE IN THEM.

It's so important to take care of yourself—emotionally, mentally, physically. This is your one life and your one body. I love to work, so it can be hard for me to focus on myself. It's easy to put my energy into work, school, and a million different tasks. But I'm starting to chase beautiful moments in life. I feel like there's pressure on all of us to always be "on" because of social media and how everyone looks like they have the perfect life. I forget to listen to my body and give myself what I need. I'm striving to get better at it. Yesterday afternoon, I was putting down my work for the day when I noticed that the sun was setting. I put on shoes and ran outside to this spot in my neighborhood where I used to go with my childhood best friend. I sat on the ground, played some music, and just watched the sunset. It was perfect.

Take those chances when you can. Find the beauty and the peace in small moments every day. We all move so fast, and disconnecting and making time for yourself to do a few yoga poses, journal, listen to music, or go for a walk can be so healthy and centering. That's how you reconnect to yourself and to the world around you.

BE SPONTANEOUS.
DON'T BE AFRAID
TO LET LOOSE, LAUGH,
AND ACT GOOFY.

The best nights are almost always the spontaneous ones. I'm such a planner and I'm hyperorganized with my schedule, so just seeing where a night takes me is one of my favorite ways to spend time. It's when I get to turn my brain off and accept things as they come. I love when my friends call and say, "I'll pick you up in ten minutes." We'll go out and drive around until we decide what we want to do—going out to eat, playing mini golf, or doing something outside the box, like visiting a haunted house around Halloween or an escape room. It helps me live in the moment and not take anything too seriously. My friends bring out the loud, goofy person in me and help me get out of my head. Some of my favorite memories are of going down to a park in town with my friends and just running around, screaming and laughing and chasing each other. I find a lot of value in freeing up brain space to be goofy, relax, and recharge.

YOU CAN MAKE
MORE MONEY,
BUT YOU CAN'T MAKE
MORE TIME.

Recently, I was offered a role in a movie that I was excited about. I was finishing up filming in Spain for part of the summer, and I was dying to get home and visit my family, who I hadn't seen in three months. This new gig meant going directly to work and not seeing them. It was a great opportunity and I was grateful for it, but I knew that I needed to reconnect with my family and friends. That felt like a bigger priority to me. As much as I love my work, and as much as I put my all into everything I do, my number one priority is God, then family, friends, and school.

It's common for young actors to work all the time and say yes to every opportunity. But they forget there are bigger things in their lives than work. It's a hard business because it's so inconsistent, and it's tough to stop the ball when it's rolling. But you have to pace yourself. And you always need to have a reason you accept a new job. That way, you're holding your work to a high standard and truly choosing the projects that speak to you, your values, and your goals for your career. I encourage all of you to think about why you're doing the things you're doing and ask yourself: *Is it worth it?* Because at the end of the day, your mental health and well-being are paramount.

TO HEAR WHAT YOUR
BODY NEEDS, YOU NEED
TO GET QUIET FIRST.

I used to think rest was a waste of time, because I just wanted to work. I have to remind myself that rest is essential to my productivity. To do my best work and stay healthy, I've got to take time to recharge. I write out a schedule for my day on my phone, and I build in time to lie in bed and rest, or even to play some music and sit on my lawn. Taking that time to be still is so important, and it took me a while to prioritize it.

When you're not resting, you're not 100 percent. If you're working so hard that you're sacrificing your free time and health, you should ask yourself if you're doing your best work. What's the point of working yourself to the bone if you won't be happy with the outcome? If you want to be productive and effective and successful, you can't burn yourself out.

LISTEN TO YOUR INTUITION,
AND DON'T BE AFRAID
TO SAY NO.

These days I'm a little more selective about choosing projects. I want to build a certain body of work, and if that means turning down jobs, that's what I'm going to do, because I want nothing more than to be passionate about my work. When it comes to signing on to new projects, like a big movie that could boost my recognition, I'm not automatically saying yes. When I invest so much of my time and energy, it should be for something that I'll feel proud of for the rest of my life. Be selective.

THE TRICK TO AVOIDING
UNNECESSARY STRESS
IS TO MIND YOUR OWN
BUSINESS.

There are so many problems in the world, and unless it's about outright injustice, bullying, or hate, you're often better off staying out of it. You know who you are as a person and what your intentions are, so don't get caught up in the drama. It took me so long to learn this, but I finally realized that no one else's opinion matters to me but my family's. When it comes to social drama and gossip, never combat negative energy with more negative energy. You won't get anywhere. Don't underestimate the value of not saying anything at all. Don't spend your energy working up a good clapback. You're lowering yourself. It's better to let things be.

If you have big plans and big dreams, little dramas are just not worth putting your energy into. It's better to focus on the things that make you happy, your goals and priorities. When negative things inevitably come your way, show the world how you handle them with grace.

YOU CAN'T CONTROL
EVERY SITUATION,
BUT YOU CAN CONTROL
HOW YOU REACT TO
THE SITUATION.

You are responsible for how you react to tough situations. I had drama with a girl who was spreading false rumors about me because she thought I had a thing with her ex. She's a fellow actress in Hollywood: successful, powerful, experienced. I had never met her, yet she had it out for me. She spun lies to mutual friends and industry acquaintances, hurting my image and my ability to make friends.

Finally, I opened up to Enrique, my mom, and some friends about what was going on. They all said the same thing: you cannot let this girl affect your life. I felt a weight lift off my shoulders. I couldn't control her or stop her from talking about me. The only thing I could control was myself. Though we had many mutual friends, this girl and I had no friendship to salvage. I just rode it out because I didn't want to waste my time and energy creating even more drama. And eventually, we all moved on.

If you react to difficult circumstances with a negative mindset, you're going to lose control and feel victimized. But if you react with determination and positivity, you can try to fix the situation. And if it can't be fixed, you can let go of what you can't control and move forward. You can't keep people from putting negativity out there, but you *can* control the energy you're devoting to it and how it affects your life.

YOU CAN'T BE ALL THINGS
TO ALL PEOPLE. YOU CAN
ONLY BE WHO YOU ARE.

There's so much pressure for teenagers to excel at school, to embrace their interests and push themselves to be the best, and to look ahead to the future with certainty. With access to so much information, so many potential career paths, and the world of social media and influencers, it can be overwhelming. We're blessed to live in a culture where individuality and unique interests are cherished and valued. But sometimes all the pressure makes "being yourself" turn into work. I struggled with managing my work as an actress and my school work, and my deeply ingrained desire to do well at both. Plus, I worried about my image and how I was leading my young fans who follow me on social media. I stressed about reviews, auditions, what my peers said about me, and if I was living up to the big stakes of my Hollywood career. It wasn't until I really connected to my inner voice and my instincts that I began to see and honor who I am as a person, and everything else fell into place. It wasn't hard to know what to say, what to do, what to wear when I was being myself. If I listened to my inner compass, I would never go in the wrong direction.

DO WHAT FEELS RIGHT
TO YOU AND IGNORE
OUTSIDE PRESSURES.

The people I admire most are those who break boundaries and listen to their hearts despite feeling pressure to do things a certain way or follow the herd. People get so caught up in trying to fit in that they either make poor decisions for other people's approval or become like everyone else, forfeiting their individuality. In the last few years, I have worked on believing in myself and getting comfortable listening to my instincts. The powers that be influence young people to conform—to wear, like, listen to, and think the same things. But I say, follow your heart. Do what feels good and right, and ignore everything else. Dress how you want to dress, listen to music you love regardless of anyone else's taste, and take piano lessons if you've always wanted to tickle the ivories.

IT'S YOUR BODY.
WHAT YOU CHOOSE
TO DO WITH IT IS
FOR YOU TO DECIDE.

Having sex means something different to everyone. There's no need to worry about somebody else's beliefs, values, or ideas. It's always going to be there, waiting for you when you're ready. Just because other people are doing it doesn't mean you need to try it to be included. At the end of the day, that's your business, and nobody else's

Take it from me: Be confident in whatever feels right to you. You don't owe anyone—even someone you love—an explanation for why you don't want to do what they want. Be clear and direct when you're talking about what you're comfortable with. You both have to engage, and it needs to be face to face. If you're not on the same page, and the other person wants to do something that you're not ready for, then you may have to go your separate ways—and that is okay.

EMBRACE
YOUR AMBITION

YOUR IMAGINATION
IS YOUR SUPERPOWER.

Your imagination is everything. Embrace your unique stories and ideas, and don't be afraid to share them with the world—you never know what could be possible. When my younger brother was about eight years old, he had to give a school presentation on an activity he loved. He was allowed to write an essay, make a PowerPoint, or draw a diagram. Marcus knew he wanted his to be different from the rest of the class's projects, but he didn't know how. He decided to write a song about camping, and he used the music of a Bruno Mars song to set his original lyrics against. Then he practiced and practiced. Marcus is the funniest person at home but was always quiet at school. This experience encouraged him to put himself out there. He ended up getting an A+, and the teacher said that it was the best presentation she'd seen in years. It gave him more confidence moving forward, and it's something I remind myself of when I'm feeling hesitant to share myself with the world.

DON'T LET ANYONE
DISCOURAGE YOU FROM
FOLLOWING YOUR DREAMS.

Growing up, I was bullied for having the big dream of making it as an actress. A lot of people, whether they were envious or believed I couldn't do it, made fun of me. They said I was full of myself or conceited, and they criticized my appearance. I was a bit of a late bloomer, so kids called me "table," among other stupid names, because I was flat-chested. They said I wasn't hot enough to be on TV or in the movies.

Of course this hurt my feelings, but even though all these mean things were being said about me, I had to stay true to myself. I knew what I was doing. I knew I was working in Hollywood and gaining traction. I didn't feel the need to rub it in other people's faces. I put my head down and worked hard. I kept doing my thing at school, auditioned, and put everything into pursuing my dream. I knew I couldn't change their minds, so I just channeled my energy into my goals, and ultimately I proved those people wrong. What mattered was the satisfaction of knowing I put my mind to something and accomplished it.

AS YOU BECOME
MORE SUCCESSFUL,
PEOPLE ALONG THE
WAY WILL TRY TO BREAK
YOU. JUST KILL 'EM
WITH KINDNESS AND
KEEP RISING.

There will always be negative people who don't want you to succeed. Anytime you're being bullied, just think about how unhappy those people must be. Angry people can't be happy, and I pray for them to find their happiness and learn to love themselves. For people who comment online and put negativity out there, they know they'll never see your face—hiding behind a screen emboldens them. And often they're looking for attention to deal with their own insecurities. Focus on the highlights of *your* life, and when things bring you down, simply acknowledge them and then move forward.

DON'T OVERTHINK.

It's often difficult for me to make decisions, and I struggle with that every day. I overthink decisions big and small, even something like posting a photo on Instagram. I'm trying to learn to trust my instincts more.

After *Stuck in the Middle* ended, I was supposed to test for the lead in a new Netflix show, and my agents asked, "Is this a project you want to do? Is this where you see your career going?" The Netflix show was an over-the-top comedy, very much in line with *Stuck in the Middle*. I wanted to try something different, and when I listened to my gut, the project felt wrong. My mom couldn't get over the fact that I'd turned down a great job as the lead on a show. But when the show came out, I knew I'd made the right decision: It wasn't me, and it wasn't where I wanted my career to go. For a few months after, though, I didn't book anything, and I got really in my head about it. I even wondered if I should continue acting. Then the opportunity for *You* came along, and it was the perfect role to push me in exactly the ways I wanted. If I hadn't listened to my gut and turned down that other show, I wouldn't have been able to do *You*.

CRITICISM IS A WAY TO GET STRONGER, BETTER, AND SMARTER—UNLESS YOU MAKE IT THE REASON WHY YOU QUIT.

I used to be terrible at receiving criticism, especially when it came to my work. I saw it as an attack on my character and who I was as a person, rather than one person's opinion about my job. Ultimately, that attitude was part of the reason I wasn't improving as an actress.

I've worked on taking critique in the spirit of somebody who's trying to learn and grow every day. My dad reminds me that it's always okay to make mistakes, as long as you embrace them, accept accountability, and use them as tools to get better. You're never too old to learn, and criticism is help and direction toward becoming better—however hard it is to hear sometimes. Without criticism, you could get stuck and stop growing. We all need it to improve. If you think you can do no wrong, then you're just setting yourself up for failure. That's on you.

LET GO OF YOUR EGO.

When you have a huge ego, you're creating an unrealistic idea of yourself in your head. There are billions of people on Earth, and there's been a flow of life for millions of years. Yes, you are special and unique, but you are not above anyone else. Your life—and your success—is a combination of hard work, timing, and opportunity.

When you let go of your ego, when you're humble and open-minded, you're in a better position to improve, to learn, to grow, to absorb what's happening around you and not to be so confident that you think you know everything. When you're egotistical, you hold back your growth, whereas being humble exposes you to new ideas, to learning more and working toward becoming the best you can be.

Reading audition sides in front of my family is an especially humbling experience. When I'm going for big roles, my parents suggest that I read my lines with the whole family so they can give me notes. I get nervous reading lines in front of them because they are honest with me in a way that no one else is. They know me well, and their feedback comes from the perspective of fans and viewers, not industry insiders. It's usually spot on, and as embarrassing as reading for my family can be, I tend to book the jobs they help me prepare for.

LIVE EVERY DAY WITH
A GRATEFUL HEART.

I'm super grateful and very fortunate to have opportunities that other people haven't been given. I never take anything for granted. I just happened to be born two hours away from LA, and my mom just happened to have a follower on Facebook who ended up being the casting director who helped me get into the business. That is luck. And I will never forget it. So many kids may not have the same proximity or opportunity or support to pursue their dreams. When people get very egotistical, very big-headed, and forget where they came from, they pull away from their roots and overlook how lucky they are. I try to stay grounded, focus on my gratitude for the ability to do what I love every day.

CREATIVITY IS THE LIGHT
THAT LEADS YOU THROUGH
THE DARK TIMES.

I'm most inspired to write or work when I'm feeling down. During that period in my life when I was depressed and *very* sad all the time, I just wanted to lie in this black hole I had created for myself. I believed that I was never going to be good enough, that my life was never going to be perfect enough. I put tremendous pressure on myself, and I couldn't bear the possibility of failing. I thought that I'd hurt my family by failing them and that I'd become a disappointment. That was my fear for months and months. I find that depression is something that you carry for the rest of your life and learn to live with in some form.

Sometimes I'll hear certain things or think certain thoughts that take me back to that time. Anytime these thoughts come rushing back, I tell myself to get up, do something, start writing a script, work on something. I don't want to be there again, and that's what helps me. When I sit there in my sadness, it becomes a pit of misery that I get stuck in. That's why I get most creative when I'm down, because it's my motivation to keep going.

APPRECIATE WHERE YOU

ARE AND ENJOY

THE JOURNEY

AS YOU WORK TOWARD

WHERE YOU'RE GOING.

I think about the future *constantly*. It's so easy to compare yourself to others, and it can be hard for me to appreciate my own success and my hard-earned progress when others are on their own (sometimes faster) trajectory. When I see another young actress book a terrific, buzzy movie or TV show that launches her career in a huge way, I can't help thinking how long it took me to book something similar, or how I want to achieve the same kind of high-profile role.

Acting is a career of comparison and competition. I am always aware of what others are doing, especially as a young woman of color. There are fewer roles written with an actor like me in mind, and I have to earn roles that aren't necessarily intended for me. This can be either tough or motivating, depending on the day, but it's a part of the job.

Seven years into my career, I often think about what I haven't accomplished yet. I tend to see my work as a race with myself. I don't always take the time to step back and reflect on how far I've come and how much I've grown. This year, I've worked hard to stay in the present. I'm striving now more than ever to truly appreciate what I've accomplished, and to consider every step toward my goals as part of a beautiful, growth-filled journey.

LIFE IS TOO SHORT TO SIT AROUND AND WAIT FOR OPPORTUNITIES TO COME TO YOU. SOMETIMES YOU HAVE TO OPEN DOORS YOURSELF.

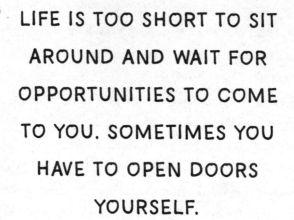

On one particular occasion when I was told that I didn't get another big movie I'd auditioned for, I was devastated. I'd gone on several rounds and poured my heart into the role. It had been down to the wire, and when I heard the news, I thought, *Well, that's another door shut in my face.* My family comforted me by reminding me how many future roles would come my way.

I kept thinking about how I could turn this apparent failure into an opportunity. I'd always wanted to try writing, producing, and directing, and this seemed like the perfect time to start. Instead of waiting for new projects to come my way, I took the initiative and threw myself into the creative process of writing and developing my own project.

Right now, I have about twenty different, incomplete scripts on Final Draft, and I love having an outlet for the inspirations that strike me everywhere and anywhere. Working on my own projects gives me an injection of hope. Some of the greatest success stories are self-made creators putting themselves out there with projects that catapulted them into the next level. Don't wait for permission.

THE FUTURE IS
WHAT YOU MAKE IT,
SO DREAM BIG.

Big dreams help you discover who you are and open up a world of possibilities. By going out and chasing your dreams, you're setting yourself up for a lifetime of happiness where you see your goals become realities. I'm a prime example of how dreaming big can pay off. A lot of girls want to be actresses, but not everyone turns it into a reality. My career is the result of dreaming big.

Growing up, I wanted to be an astronaut, then the first female president, then an actress. Acting was accessible, and it was something I could accomplish immediately. After I announced that it was what I wanted to do, the stubborn side of me took hold. That's where the hard work came in. My parents always believed in me and supported me, but this was a pretty far-fetched dream for an eight-year-old from the Coachella Valley. I took it as my opportunity to prove people wrong, which I love to do. I began educating myself, watching as many movies as I could, practicing in the mirror, performing for friends and family, and praying. It was still a long shot that was made possible by my parents supporting me and some really good luck. But the point is this: there's no disadvantage to dreaming big, and if you deny yourself those dreams, then your life will be smaller.

SHOOTING STARS

BURN OUT FAST.

In the entertainment industry, I've noticed some actors work hard for years to find success, and others blow up right away. Many people want that immediate, undeniable success. It's not about who gets there quickest, but about who is growing into their skills and building a career they're proud of. I think it's important to remember that shooting stars burn out fast. When I think *I've been at this for five years, and all of a sudden, this actor or that actor is getting the jobs I want,* I remember actors like Nicole Kidman or Viola Davis. They worked for a long time before they got all the recognition they deserved. Life is about longevity. Be patient and never stop moving toward your goal.

Every now and then, someone or something will let me know that I've made a difference. My dad and I were walking around a shopping center the other day, and I overheard a guy say to his friends, "Oh, that's Jenna Ortega." It's unbelievable to have people know my name. Most of the time, I live in my own world and feel nothing has changed from being a little girl. Those moments take me out of my bubble and remind me I'm doing something very public, something that touches people far and wide. It's heartwarming to know people out there are supportive of me and my career, and I could not be more grateful.

WITHOUT SOMEONE
TO LOOK UP TO,
WHAT IS THERE
TO BUILD UP TO?

Having a role model—or many—is a great way to stay inspired to become your best self. Seeing the successes achieved and the risks taken by my role models has encouraged me to think big. But role models aren't just celebrities; they're people you admire and respect for their work ethic and their character.

I consider Gina Rodriguez one of my biggest role models. I met her when I was eleven and playing the younger version of her character on *Jane the Virgin*. She took time to hang out and connect with me on set. She gave me the most encouraging, supportive advice about staying true to myself, being prepared, and never getting discouraged. She told me, "I'm so proud of you. We're on this journey together." Every time I see her, she still gives me great advice.

Seeing a young Latina actress find success meant so much to me. Growing up, I could count the number of well-known Latinx actors on two hands. Not seeing people who looked like me or who I could relate to on TV was hard and discouraging. If you're inspired by someone, it leads you to ask yourself how you can turn your passion into something meaningful. It's important to look up to someone, admire the good they do, and get inspired to make an impact in your own life.

LOVE YOURSELF

YOU ONLY HAVE ONE LIFE.
TAKE RISKS AND EXPRESS
YOUR TRUE SELF
INSTEAD OF HIDING
BEHIND WHAT YOU THINK
EVERYONE ELSE WANTS.

It can feel like there's a lot of pressure to fit into a particular mold, but this is the time in our lives to step out and try new things. Enjoy yourself! Be an individual! There's nothing wrong with taking chances when it comes to beauty and style. It's a great form of self-expression, and it's okay to be different from everyone else. Be confident in your own taste. For example, when I'm home and not working, I like to be comfortable above all else. I wear baggy T-shirts, sweatpants, and my favorite hoodies. Nothing is better to me than comfort.

When I do dress up, for work or for premieres, I like things that are pretty different from what I'd usually wear. My more formal fashion style is very outside the box and pushes me out of my comfort zone. My style icons are the people who really push the envelope and take fashion to the next level, like Zendaya, Billy Porter, and Lady Gaga. I truly appreciate the way they tell stories with fashion! I'm more tomboy than anything. I'm not attracted to feminine clothes, pretty pinks or bows. I love Gwen Stefani's edgy rocker style, and I too prefer sleek, structured looks.

WEAR WHAT YOU WANT WITH CONFIDENCE.

One of the most successful fashion risks I ever took was in 2017 at the *Spider Man: Homecoming* premiere. As Enrique and I were reviewing outfit options the night before, I wasn't feeling excited about any of them. He showed me an interesting pants outfit, but it seemed a little plain. The fitted black pants were paired with a white one-shoulder top, plus a funky, studded stack-heeled sandal. I liked it in theory, but I wasn't sure it was the right look for a Marvel movie premiere. I knew there had to be something more young and fun. That gave my brilliant stylist the idea to have his artist friend spray-paint the shirt with the word "SHOOK" in a comic-book-style word bubble. We did it, totally unsure how it would look.

When the outfit came back from the artist, I loved it, but I got self-conscious that I couldn't pull it off and it would draw too much attention at a premiere for a movie I wasn't even in. But Enrique convinced me to take the risk. I was worried that it was too on theme and too out there, but I ended up really loving the outfit!

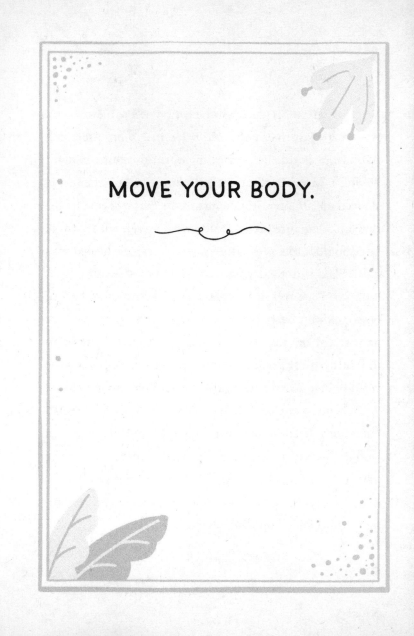

MOVE YOUR BODY.

You have to take care of your body, but you can experiment and decide what works for you. Playing outside, exercising, and connecting with loved ones are all great ways to engage your body and your confidence. When I get too busy, I tend to let exercise drop off my schedule, and then I feel like even more of a mess. When I work out regularly—even light exercise in my room or a quick jog around the neighborhood—I feel better, calmer, accomplished. That's the beauty of endorphins.

The hardest part is making the decision to exercise. But then you'll feel so good and proud. Sometimes it's easiest just to put your shoes on. Even if you procrastinate after that, you'll probably go out and do something once you're all laced up. Use that momentum!

THE PRETTIEST THING

A GIRL CAN WEAR

IS HER CONFIDENCE.

I've long struggled with my self-confidence, and I used to be very insecure. I'd look at girls on social media and be so envious of how good they looked. The more I stared at their pictures, the more I realized they all had one thing in common: confidence. As long as you hold your head high, people are going to think you look great. And more important, you'll feel it in yourself.

The truth is that until you truly feel confident in your own skin and in your own life, you won't be able to make your mark as an individual. I realized that looking at the beautiful photos of influencers and style icons on social media was sparking insecurity in me. I started spending less time there so that I could focus more on myself. And when I feel good about what I'm doing, then I can be more supportive of others without envy.

THE MORE TIME
WE SPEND ON
SOCIAL MEDIA, THE MORE
WE CHIP AWAY AT OUR
OWN SELF-ESTEEM.

We live in a culture where not seeming glamorous enough or being exciting enough is looked down on. Unrealistic standards are praised with cringey comments like "You betta werkkk!" or "Super snatched!" (Typing those words just made my soul leave my body.) People grow attached to the comments, loving the instant positive feedback, but their feelings are hurt if they don't get that same level of praise every time. This motivates them to try harder, spending more time on social media paying attention to what's doing well and what isn't.

We crave approval from others and stalk people-we-wish-we-could-be accounts. If only we could look like them, be funny like them, have an amazingly fun life like them.

I try not to put a lot of value on what happens on social media. I don't worry about how many likes or comments a post gets—as long as I make content I can stand by, I feel good. No one's opinion matters to me as much as my family's and close friends', even though I'm happy to have a positive community of followers. I am grateful for everyone's support, and all I can do is spread love and light, be true to myself, and do what makes me happy.

YOU ARE ENOUGH

JUST THE WAY

YOU ARE.

There's so much pressure to "be yourself," like those Instagram accounts that choose the exact right filter to make their pictures look natural. There's an expectation that "being yourself" is never going out without at least some makeup on. Heaven forbid somebody knows you have a zit. But you don't need the makeup. You don't need the filter. You're not perfect, and your life isn't perfect, because nobody's is. But who you are and what you do is *enough*.

ALWAYS BE
THE BEST VERSION
OF *YOU*, INSTEAD OF
TRYING TO BE
ANY VERSION
OF SOMEONE ELSE.

When I started out on social media, I was maybe eleven or twelve—probably younger than I should have been, but it felt important for my job. I started following all these people who were suggested for me or who my friends followed: influencers, beauty experts, a few comedians, various online personalities. I was floored seeing their posts, how many followers they had, and how beautiful and perfect they all seemed. I wasn't insecure yet, but I was so easily influenced by what I saw these other people doing. I began to think that I should try to dress like them, or look like them, or tell jokes in the same way.

But it just wasn't working for me. I was piecing together a persona and a look that didn't fit with my personality. Sometimes I'd repeat jokes from Instagram or YouTube to see what my family thought, and they'd go silent and look at each other like, *What is going on?* I had to learn that you can appreciate other people's talents and appearances, and even draw inspiration from them, but that should supplement your natural identity instead of replacing it. Explore what you like, keep trying new things, discover what you love—but don't ever bury what you already know to be true.

LOVING YOURSELF
IS A JOURNEY.

It doesn't happen overnight—we all have insecurities. When I was younger, I was a ham: performing, seeking attention, being goofy, and loving it. But around the age of thirteen, I didn't like anything about myself. I started questioning how I looked, how I acted. I was so busy questioning everything that I lost sight of who I really was for a while. Now I'm on the journey back to knowing and loving myself. I am committed to learning something new about myself every day. Some things I like, and some things I want to work on. I'm not always confident, and I'm by no means perfect. But even in that journey to improve and grow, I'm finding love for myself. Loving yourself means coming to terms with your insecurities and so-called flaws, and learning to embrace and celebrate them.

IT'S OKAY TO BE BLESSED

IN SO MANY WAYS

AND STILL STRUGGLE.

IT'S OKAY TO

NOT BE OKAY.

When I first went to my therapist and really talked to someone about my feelings, I was embarrassed. I felt like I didn't deserve to complain or feel sad. There are people whose lives are much harder than mine, so what right did I have to be depressed? I had a hard time opening up to the therapist because I didn't want her to think of me as ungrateful or whiny. I cared so much what others thought that I almost preferred feeling bad to being judged by my therapist. But we can't think about it that way. We're all entitled to our feelings.

Let's allow ourselves to have bad days. Be patient with yourself, but take action to seek help. It took a lot for me to acknowledge to my therapist how I was feeling, but in hindsight, I am so grateful I did. The journey to happiness or recovery or peace may be long, but it can't begin until you ask for help and start doing the work.

LABELS ARE LIMITS.

All my life, I've been saddled with labels, whether it was being a girl interested in "different" sports or politics, or later as a young actress with an outspoken stance on social justice issues.

When I was little, I wanted to be the first female president, and people told me "no way." You know, because "girls can't be president." For a long time I believed in the labels because I was fed them for years and they became ingrained in me. It wasn't until I got older that I realized I don't have to let labels and limits prevent me from trying new experiences, pushing boundaries, or engaging with new people.

The pressure to fit into a certain box can stunt your creativity. But you're in control of your life, and you get to decide which people to surround yourself with, the way you want to look, and what passions you want to pursue. Now that I've given up on these labels, I like to look at everybody as limitless.

STOP COMPARING
YOURSELF TO OTHERS.
YOU ARE YOURSELF, AND
THAT'S SOMETHING
THEY CAN NEVER BE.

People are too hard on themselves. For those who have low self-esteem, comparison to others is toxic. And to believe that you can't measure up in some way can be isolating. It's important to be honest about this, because so many people are going through the same thing—even people who you think are absolutely perfect. And who's to say that other people aren't looking at you and wondering how *they* compare?

WHAT REALLY MATTERS
IS WHAT YOU PUT OUT
INTO THIS WORLD—
YOUR ENERGY,
YOUR PERSONALITY,
YOUR KINDNESS.

I can't stand materialism. When I started working and spending more time in LA, one of the first designer pieces I bought for myself was a very high-end backpack. But here's the thing: I didn't care about the bag. The only reason I got it was because I felt pressured to buy it. The friend I was with encouraged me to get it, saying I'd be going to events and should look nice and put together. My mom joined in and encouraged me, too, saying I never treat myself. So I bought it—which was truly *dumb*. How many times have you met someone and thought, *Oh, wow, she has really nice things. I bet she's a great person!* NEVER. The greatest people you'll meet in life are the people you connect with and who you feel are honest and genuine. It has nothing to do with what bag they carry, or what shoes they're wearing, or what's hanging in their closets. Buy and wear what makes you happy.

NOBODY KNOWS
WHAT'S BETTER FOR YOU
THAN YOU.

Let's say you're talking to somebody you're super into. And because you're nervous, you're not sure how to reply to a text message they've sent. So you do what so many of us do, which is ask five friends to give you their opinions. Before you know it, you're writing a response as a group and crowd-sourcing every word and emoji.

This is the perfect chance to make your own decisions. Be confident in responding to your crush with whatever comes to mind. If they engage further and appreciate your sense of humor, then that's a genuine connection! If not, maybe it's not meant to be. But you'll never know that if your best friend is the one texting with them.

You have to trust yourself. This is coming from somebody who spent a lot of years putting other people's ideas and opinions and ideology before her own instincts. But I've learned that nobody knows what's better for you than you.

BELIEVE
IN YOUR POWER

I CARE.

YOU SHOULD, TOO.

In June 2018, I attended the Radio Disney Music Awards and wore one of the most controversial outfits of my life. I was hosting part of the awards, and I knew it was an opportunity to use media attention to spotlight an injustice I was upset about. At the time, news about our country's immigration detention centers was breaking, and First Lady Melania Trump visited the camps wearing a jacket that said "I really don't care, do you?" I found it inappropriate and heartless. I was planning to wear a similar military-style green jacket to the show, so I worked with my stylist to come up with a fashion response. My jacket featured this on the back: "I do care and u should too."

I needed to share this message on a big stage. I care deeply about others, and I care deeply about the detainees held in centers along the Mexican border. I received some negative comments from viewers, but there was a lot of positive feedback, too. Most people avoid talking about these issues in fear of offending anyone or losing support. I encourage my fans to speak up for what they believe in. We're not able to effect change without using our voices.

OUR VOICES ARE A
POWERFUL TOOL
FOR CHANGE.
SO IS OUR SILENCE.

In 2018, I went on an incredible trip to Kenya with the WE organization, a nonprofit devoted to transforming lives through social change domestically and internationally. We traveled to Kenya because many communities there don't have access to clean water, and many children don't have access to education. WE works to raise money and build infrastructure for clean water wells and schools, and I was fortunate to be one of their volunteers on this trip.

It was a life-changing experience that put things into perspective for me. We worked on bringing awareness to the importance of accessible water supplies and education, and we built schools ourselves, working with the community to mix and pour the concrete. It's easy to forget how fortunate I am, taking basic needs like clean water for granted. Until I made the trek alongside some Kenyan women, I had never thought about the daily challenge of having to walk miles for water that wasn't even clean.

After we got back to the United States, WE organized a day of silence to raise awareness about the issues in Kenya. All the volunteers, supporters, and ambassadors stayed away from public appearances and social media, instead reflecting on privilege and how we can help others.

PEOPLE OF ALL
DIFFERENT COLORS
AND BACKGROUNDS
SHOULD SEE THEMSELVES
REPRESENTED.

When I was little, I didn't see much diversity on-screen. I watched Dakota Fanning and admired her acting skills and thought, *I could be the Latina Dakota Fanning.* When I envisioned becoming an actress, I thought I'd have to be the Latina version of someone else. Just being me wasn't an option.

When I had the opportunity to voice Princess Isabel on Disney's animated *Elena of Avalor,* I never dreamed that Elena would be the Latina role model I'd dreamed of. The full impact of the character didn't hit me until I went to Walt Disney World, when they were debuting Elena in the parks. She was going to be a character greeting young fans, and they were selling Elena-themed dresses and merchandise. I saw little kids of all colors lining up to meet her and buying the dolls and toys. A few days later in Target, I saw a girl holding an Elena doll, jumping up and down and saying, "She looks like me!" The joy on that girl's face meant the world to me.

When I was four years old, I asked my mom if I could dye my hair blond so I could look like Cinderella. But this generation will have a Disney Princess who looks like them. It's both a point of pride for me and a point of personal healing that I was able to give that to young girls.

INVITE PEOPLE
TO SHARE THEIR TRUTH
WITH YOU.

Lots of people in LA, and Hollywood specifically, try to tell you what you want to hear. One day I was on set and I asked for feedback on a scene. Whenever the writer is on set, I get their thoughts—I want to make sure I'm delivering the performance they had in mind. In this case, the writer would only give me compliments. That's not helpful for me! The writer crafts the story, and I want to make sure I deliver on their vision so we can collaborate to get an end product we're all proud of. That doesn't happen if people bite their tongue and avoid saying something important.

EMBRACE YOUR
DIFFERENCES. SURROUND
YOURSELF WITH THOSE
WHO LIFT YOU UP,
NOT BRING YOU DOWN.

When I was in middle school, I had to go to LA a lot and work. At the time, I hung out with people who made me feel bad whenever I had to leave school. They made fun of me, saying I thought I was so fancy. These were the people in my classes and my lunch period, who saw me every day. I didn't think I could stay away from them. It took me a while to realize how their words were infiltrating my thoughts. I always try to be the nice peacekeeper, to give someone the benefit of the doubt. After a while, though, I realized that my so-called friends were bringing me down with their constant negativity. When you surround yourself with negative energy, it can take a toll without you even realizing it. It starts to change who you are as a person.

I ended up finding new friends I loved, and I even reconnected with some old ones from elementary school. The new people in my life were positive, supportive, and genuine. They made me feel good.

EVERYONE FEELS JEALOUS.
YOUR CHARACTER
IS DEFINED
BY HOW YOU HANDLE
THAT FEELING.

To me, jealousy is such a dangerous, toxic feeling. I find that a lot of jealousy is rooted in relationships: who's dating who, which friend is invited where. I'm not always included in everything my friends are doing, and that's okay. I'm doing my own things, and I enjoy being by myself. I know that my friends and I will spend plenty of time together and support each other.

My insecurity and envy usually affect me most when it comes to my work. If someone else books a job that I want, of course I feel a pang of envy. But I don't let that emotion linger. I've learned how to turn it into motivation. If you wallow in envy, you're just wallowing in negativity. Moving past it is something I've had to practice over the years. Now it's a feeling that doesn't last more than a second. I journal to get through it. I write down positive, love-filled thoughts to remind myself that envy is a natural human emotion but also a distraction that keeps me from my true purpose.

BE THE GOOD
YOU SEEK IN OTHERS.

Stop criticizing, and focus on the good. Try to find ways to be positive. If even one person in your friend circle is positive, maybe somebody else will internalize that energy. Not that we all can't have bad days or feel off, but we're defined by what we choose to focus on and how we handle our moods. Imagine if everyone was working toward positive energy!

Last year I was driving home from LA with my mom. It was another long car trip, and I felt overwhelmed. My mom was trying to start conversations and get me to laugh, but I couldn't shake my mood. Finally, she said, "Jenna, you can be hard to be around sometimes. You can be really negative."

I was stunned. I had never seen myself that way. I'd never considered how my moods or negativity affect the people I loved. That was a life-changing moment. I knew that if my negative energy was affecting my closest relationship, it had to be affecting all my relationships. I started noticing people's energy after that, and realized how much I connect with people who are positive and outgoing, who brighten up a room by laughing and having fun. But I'd never thought of being that person for somebody else. It took me a while to figure out that I could have that energy and reflect it back for others.

IT TAKES REAL STRENGTH
TO ASK FOR HELP.

For somebody who is stubborn and often called independent, asking for help has been a tough lesson to learn.

When I first started filming *Stuck in the Middle,* I'd been in public school all my life. Once I had to be on set, I began homeschooling and working with the studio teachers. I was scared to ask for support because I didn't want to seem like I couldn't do it on my own. I started taking algebra, and though I love it now, at the time I felt so confused. I got a call from my high school math teacher, who was reviewing and evaluating my schoolwork, and she cut right to the chase: "Jenna, you're clearly having trouble understanding this. Why don't you ask your tutor for help?" I finally caved and asked my on-set teacher, who explained the concepts thoroughly and worked with me. All of a sudden my mind opened up and everything made sense.

I'd formed this idea that I was somebody who wasn't meant to ask for help, that I was too independent, self-sufficient, and grown up. Thankfully I realized that was a sign of stubbornness, not independence. There's no harm in asking for help. In fact, it's a sign of maturity and growth.

YOUR VALUE
COMES FROM WITHIN,
NOT FROM OTHERS.

Too often we let our insecurities and worries dictate who we think we are and the standards we set for ourselves. It's important to remember that nobody's life holds more value than another's. We're all going through the same things, so stop the comparisons and start supporting each other.

I once had this friend who was so sweet, talented, and beautiful. I remember feeling incredibly insecure whenever I compared myself to her. Those thoughts were making me feel bad about myself. Meanwhile, I didn't know she felt the same way about me!

I've learned to admire good qualities in others without changing the way I feel about myself. Anytime I see someone whose look I love, or who is so funny, or who has a great smile, I tell them. It makes you a more positive person, and it makes everyone feel good. Building someone else up doesn't tear you down.

LET YOUR ACTIONS
SPEAK LOUDEST.

I don't believe in hype; I believe in hard work and results. A lot of people spend a lot of energy building up new projects and hyping them, and they end up being half-baked and unworthy of all the excitement. It's easy to spend more time and energy creating hype when the project doesn't meet the high expectations you've set. It's more satisfying for me to work really hard on something without anybody knowing, and then let it speak for itself.

WHAT DO YOU WANT
TO BE REMEMBERED
FOR? TOMORROW ISN'T
PROMISED, AND THE
THINGS THAT YOU DO NOW
WILL BE HOW PEOPLE
REMEMBER YOU.

When you're young, you think that you can do anything you want, that you have plenty of time to mature and eventually become the person you want to be. But how you treat people, how you act, is who you are. And that's how you'll be remembered.

When I'm on set and working hard, I can get caught up in what I need to do to be my best, and I can take for granted all the help and work going on around me. Which is why I make it a priority to thank every crew member and production assistant who is working hard at their job so that I can work hard at my job. I express my gratitude all the time. I consider how I want to be remembered, which means I think about my actions more. And I try not to take anything for granted, because I know it could all be taken from me in an instant.

SPEAK OUT TO MAKE
POSITIVE CHANGE,
NO MATTER HOW
DIFFICULT THE SUBJECT,
HOW HIGH THE STAKES,
OR HOW BIG THE STAGE.

In 2017, I spoke at the United Nations about my experience with the UNAIDS organization bringing more awareness to HIV. I delivered my speech to a room of world leaders, diplomats, and activists. It was nerve-racking to speak with the prime minister of Uganda sitting to my left and the president of France to my right. There were many speeches that day, most about data and statistics, while I spoke from the heart about my grandfather's death from AIDS and the toll it's taken on my family. It's something I hadn't spoken about publicly, but I knew it was an opportunity to share the effect of this illness on us.

My grandfather passed away before I was born. He was an entertainer and came out as gay later in life. I feel a deep connection with him because I got his knack for performing. As I was speaking at the UN, I began to cry from the emotion of the moment. I felt so vulnerable, standing onstage as the youngest person in the room. As I continued speaking, attendees put their forks down to look up at the stage. The side chatter slowed, then stopped. After my speech, one of the foreign ministers who had initially paid me no mind came up and asked to continue the conversation. That was a big day for me. I felt that I lived up to the enormous stakes of the event, and that was what truly mattered.

YOU CAN DO
ANYTHING YOU WANT TO.

It takes courage to explore your passions and follow your ambitions. If you've dreamed of writing a novel, if you've fantasized about writing and performing an original song, if making captain of your soccer team is your ideal—go for it. You may not have all the resources available right now, or all the knowledge or skills you need, but you can start. And who knows—you may start writing music or taking acting classes and realize it's not for you. But through that experience, you'll learn about hard work and practice, and maybe meet new friends who will introduce you to another cool activity. Putting yourself out there is always a good idea. Experiment and educate yourself as much as possible.

The thought of failing can be scary and intimidating, but going after your dream is so worthwhile. Never let your fears stop you from working toward your goals. You are in charge of your story. Don't let anybody else write it for you.

ABOUT THE AUTHOR

JENNA ORTEGA is an award-winning actress and media personality. In addition to starring in Jennifer Garner's *Yes Day, Elena of Avalor, Jane the Virgin,* and Netflix's *You* and *The Babysitter 2,* Jenna partners with the National Bullying Prevention Center and the AIDS Healthcare Foundation, and she is also the new face of Neutrogena. When not acting, Jenna spends her time discussing Latinx representation in media, writing screenplays, and being with her family in the Coachella Valley.

@JennaOrtega